MW01702947

Specific Skill Series
for Language Arts

Paragraphs

Leveled Books in Nine Key Language Arts Skill Areas

SRA

Columbus, OH

The McGraw-Hill Companies

Cover: ©Tim Flach/Getty Images, Inc.

SRAonline.com

SRA

Send all inquiries to:
SRA/McGraw-Hill
8787 Orion Place
Columbus, OH 43240-4027

Printed in the United States of America.

ISBN 0-07-601707-9

3 4 5 6 7 8 9 RHR 14 13 12 11 10

TO THE TEACHER

GENERAL INFORMATION ON PARAGRAPHS

Writers need to understand and apply the rules governing paragraphs in order to write effectively. A piece of writing with correct paragraphing helps the reader by breaking up long sections of prose and arranging ideas into more easily comprehended units. Writing strong paragraphs involves knowing that most paragraphs require a topic sentence and supporting sentences and that different types of paragraphs, such as narrative, descriptive, expository, and persuasive, have different purposes.

Common problems students have when writing paragraphs include the following:

- **Too short:** Paragraphs that contain only one to three normal sentences seem choppy and interruptive to the reader.
- **Too long:** Students who write overly long paragraphs might not understand the conventional structure of paragraphs.
- **Incoherence:** These paragraphs skip from idea to idea with no logical framework.

ABOUT *SPECIFIC SKILL SERIES FOR LANGUAGE ARTS*

Specific Skill Series for Language Arts is a companion to ***Specific Skill Series,*** a supplemental reading program that has been widely recognized for its effectiveness for over thirty years. The two series are designed and organized the same. ***Specific Skill Series for Language Arts*** consists of discrete units of practice exercises that target and reinforce fundamental language-arts skills. Units in both series are presented in multiple-choice format for standardized test practice.

ABOUT *PARAGRAPHS*

The scope and sequence for Books A through H of *Paragraphs* focuses on the purposes, planning, and structure of paragraphs. The scope and sequence for each book is located on the last page of the book. Each unit includes

- **rule boxes** that explain skills related to writing paragraphs.
- **models** in each rule box to illustrate the skills being discussed.
- **multiple-choice exercises** for skills practice and reinforcement.

Four **Language Activity Pages** (LAPs) appear in each book. Each LAP is divided into the following four sections and reviews the skills practiced in the preceding units:

Exercising Your Skill reviews key terms and concepts.

Expanding Your Skill provides mixed practice.

Exploring Language shows how the skills apply to real-world contexts by featuring one of six forms of writing: descriptive, narrative, personal, persuasive, expository, and poetry.

Expressing Yourself includes two creative activities related to the skills. One activity is always a Work-with-a-Partner activity to encourage collaborative learning.

TO THE TEACHER

SERIES COMPONENTS

- **Student Editions:** Nine books in each level (A–H) focus on nine skill areas: *Grammar, Usage, Mechanics, Spelling, Vocabulary, Sentences, Paragraphs, Writing Process,* and *Research.*
- **Placement Test Books:** One book for each skill area includes diagnostic tests to place students in the correct level.
- **Teacher's Manual:** Primarily an answer key, the *Teacher's Manual* also includes reproducible student worksheets and further information on how to use the program, including classroom management tips.

HOW TO USE *SPECIFIC SKILL SERIES FOR LANGUAGE ARTS*

Placing Students in Levels: The scope and sequence, complexity of skills, and readability in Levels A through H correspond to Grades 1 through 8. Students may, however, be placed in any level. For example, in the second grade, a student who needs remedial work in a specific skill may be placed in Book A, an on-level student who would benefit from skills reinforcement may be placed in Book B, and an advanced student who is ready for enrichment may be placed in Book C or higher. *Placement Tests* help place students in the correct level.

Setting: This series can be used for independent study and one-on-one practice sessions, as well as in small-group and whole-class settings. It is also effective in after-school and summer-school programs.

Getting Started: Students must have notebook paper or copies of reproducible student worksheets (located in the *Teacher's Manual*) before they begin working. Remind students not to write in the books. Students may begin in any unit of any book, depending on the skill practice they need, although it is recommended that they begin with Unit 1. As they work through the units, students should record their answers on notebook paper or on the student worksheets.

Pacing: Students should be encouraged to work at their own pace, completing a few units every day or every other day.

Scoring: Teachers should score units as soon as they have been completed. Then a discussion can be held in which students justify their answer choices.

Internet Use: Some activities, especially those in *Research,* require students to use the Internet. Students' use of the Internet should be monitored closely for content appropriateness and safety.

TO THE STUDENT

This book will show you how to write a paragraph. First you will learn about three specific types of paragraphs: narrative, persuasive, and expository. Then you will learn specific ways to improve any type of paragraph you write.

In Book E *Paragraphs,* you will learn about

- Types of Paragraphs
- Paragraph Structure (Topic Sentences, Details, Closing Sentences)
- Improving Paragraphs (Staying on Topic, Transition Words)
- Writer's Craft (Figurative Language, Word Choice)

After you complete this book, you will understand the importance of staying on topic, paying attention to word choice, using transition words, and organizing your paragraphs effectively. You will also know that different types of paragraphs have different purposes. The purpose of a persuasive paragraph is to convince the reader to think, feel, or act a certain way. Below is an example of a persuasive paragraph. The writer makes a claim and provides evidence to support that claim.

TOPIC SENTENCE

A packed lunch is better because you can choose what to put in it. Most of the time, even if you like what your school is serving for lunch, the food does not taste great. The food in a packed lunch is usually better for you as well. It is also less expensive to pack your lunch. By packing a lunch, less food will be wasted since you enjoy the items that were packed. These are some of the reasons why packing a lunch for school is a good idea.

DETAILS

CLOSING SENTENCE

As you master the skills in this book, you will understand the structure of a paragraph and the elements that are necessary for writing any type of effective paragraph.

Unit 1
Narrative Paragraphs

Topic Sentences

A **paragraph** is a group of related sentences that tell about a specific topic. Writing has different purposes so there are several types of paragraphs. The purpose of a **narrative paragraph** is to tell part or all of a true or make-believe story. A narrative paragraph can also give an account of an event.

Once you have a topic, most types of paragraphs need a **topic sentence,** which shares the main idea of your paragraph. A topic sentence is often at the beginning of a paragraph, but it can be in the middle or at the end of a paragraph as long at it makes sense. A topic sentence can even be written in the form of a paragraph.

Which topic sentence best completes each narrative paragraph?

1. You will know that you are in Rock City, New York, when you get to the fork in the road. _____ A local businessman and several friends constructed the giant fork as a joke. They placed it at the intersection of two roads in the year 2000. Local authorities have allowed the fork to remain; they must have a good sense of humor.

   (A) Follow the road to the left to get to Rock City.
   (B) In this small town in upstate New York, the main street splits.
   (C) This small town in upstate New York actually has a silver fork that is thirty-one feet tall!

2. Throughout the summer, there are many soccer camps where I live. The camp I went to lasted six hours a day for five days. During the morning session, we completed dribbling, passing, and shooting drills. We also practiced "heading the ball." Then we took an hour to eat lunch and rest. In the afternoon, we formed teams and played a real soccer match. All through the week, we each got a chance to play many positions on the field. _____

   (A) I had a great experience at soccer camp last summer.
   (B) This year I would like to attend a basketball camp.
   (C) I would drink plenty of water during the day.

3. Thomas Edison is remembered for inventing the lightbulb. _____ His inventions include the automatic telegraph, the record player, and the transmitter chip used in telephones and microphones. Edison also invented the electric railway, the electric pen, the mimeograph machine, the motion picture camera, and the storage battery. He was additionally responsible for the creation of the first practical electric generator, electric sockets, switches, and paper tape. During Edison's lifetime, he patented more than a thousand inventions.

(A) His nickname was "The Wizard of Menlo Park."

(B) However, Thomas Edison invented and perfected many other useful items.

(C) He got a job as a telegraph operator at the age of sixteen.

---

4. Have you ever heard of the White Horses of Great Britain? Altogether, there are seventeen of these horses in different areas of Great Britain. _____ The oldest statue in Uffington may be more than two thousand years old! The Uffington White Horse has served as a model for the others, which were carved in the 1700s and 1800s. Located in Wiltshire, a single White Horse has a rider on its back.

(A) Some of the guards at Buckingham Palace ride white horses.

(B) The White Horses of Great Britain are not living animals; they are horse statues cut into chalk hills.

(C) According to legend, white horses represent the victory of King Alfred over the Danes.

---

5. _____ At first, Lynn was afraid to step into the time machine. She worried that it would go back in time too far or go to the wrong place, perhaps a dangerous place. Still, Lynn wanted to visit and research the century of her great-grandparents. She finally opened the door of the time machine and took a deep breath. Lynn stepped inside and turned the blinking dial to the year 1870. She closed her eyes as she pushed the button marked "Go."

(A) How many doors would your time machine have?

(B) In 1870, the president of the United States was Ulysses S. Grant.

(C) Have you ever imagined what time travel would be like or what you would do with a time machine?

Unit 2
Narrative Paragraphs

Staying on Topic

Not just in narrative paragraphs but in all types, it is important to stay on topic. Each sentence of a paragraph should relate to the main idea. If one or more sentences in a paragraph are *not* on topic, your main idea will be unclear, and a reader may become confused.

Choose the sentence from each narrative paragraph that does *not* stay on topic.

1. Rosa Parks has been called "the spark that lit the fire" under the Civil Rights movement of the 1960s. **(A)** In 1955, Rosa Parks refused a Montgomery, Alabama, bus driver's order to give up her seat on the bus for a white man. **(B)** The states of Florida, Georgia, Tennessee, and Mississippi border Alabama. She was arrested and found guilty of disturbing the peace by a judge in Alabama. **(C)** After the ordeal, Rosa Parks made a difference by continuing to challenge segregation and racism. **(D)** In the year 1996, Rosa Parks was honored with the Presidential Medal of Freedom for her involvement in and dedication to the Civil Rights movement.

2. **(A)** Science and gardening work hand-in-hand as people try to improve upon existing fruit, or even attempt to create new fruit. Not satisfied with the multitude of fruit found in nature, some gardeners have invented new fruit by a process of crossbreeding. **(B)** Therefore, in addition to a variety of citrus fruit, we now have the tangelo, a cross between a tangerine and a grapefruit. Cherry tomatoes, however, are not a cross between a cherry and a tomato, but simply a cherry-sized tomato. **(C)** For apricot lovers looking for something different, there are plumcots, a cross between a plum and an apricot, and peachcots, a cross between a peach and an apricot. **(D)** A pinch of sugar is enough to sweeten most foods. Those who like all kinds of berries might enjoy boysenberries, which are a mixture of the raspberry, blackberry, and loganberry.

Unit 2
Narrative Paragraphs

3. Long ago, there was a shoemaker who was always very busy making shoes and boots for his customers. **(A)** Late one evening, the shoemaker realized that there was only enough material to make one pair of handmade shoelaces. **(B)** The road was slippery, and we thought it might be covered with a sheer sheet of ice. **(C)** In those days, all shoe parts were made by hand because there were no machines to make them. The shoemaker measured the material and cut the thin strands needed to weave the shoelaces. **(D)** Intending to complete the laces the next day, the shoemaker polished some shoes and went to sleep.

---

4. **(A)** The treehouse my parents built for me when I was six years old can now be used by my younger sister. When I arrived at the beach, I found a smooth stretch of sand close to a shady palm tree. **(B)** I kicked off my sandals and felt the familiar softness of the sand between my toes. I had discovered this beach earlier in the summer with friends. **(C)** Preparing to bask in the sun and warm up for a few minutes before taking a swim, I unfolded my beach towel and placed it flat on the sand. **(D)** The strong ocean breeze kept whipping up the corners of my towel until I secured it with my sandals and bottle of sunscreen. With my belongings safe, it was off to the water!

---

5. **(A)** A family of tweedles lives within the walls of our house. Tweedles are mini elf-like people who are very light on their teeny, tiny feet and enjoy singing quite softly. The only way I know the tweedles are there is because a bright light glows from them as they sing. **(B)** The tweedles sing when they think my family and I are sleeping. I have often wondered if the paper clips, coins, cotton balls, and other small items that are missing around the house end up where the tweedles live. **(C)** The kitchen is downstairs next to the living room; the den is upstairs. My parents have no idea that the tweedles make their home in our house. Tweedles sleep during the day, and sometimes I think I hear them snoring. **(D)** I wonder what else the tweedles do while we are really sleeping.

Choose the sentence from each narrative paragraph that does *not* stay on topic.

6. Jesse Owens will always be considered one of track and field's greatest stars. **(A)** While on the track and field team at The Ohio State University in Columbus, Ohio, Jesse Owens persevered. One story recalls that, even though he had a pulled back muscle one week before an important track meet, Jesse was determined to compete. **(B)** In that very meet, Owens ended up tying the world record in the 100-yard dash. He applied his work ethic to most everything he did. His determination and attitude paid off as Owens competed in the Olympics of 1936. **(C)** The Ohio State University's colors are scarlet and gray. There, he earned four gold medals. **(D)** Three of Owens' medals were for foot races, and one was for the broad, or long, jump.

---

7. **(A)** Renaissance painters began a new period in art as they rediscovered the classical style of ancient Greece and Rome. Artists of the Renaissance, such as Leonardo da Vinci and Michelangelo, studied the human form to produce realistic paintings. **(B)** They also used perspective to produce a lifelike appearance of depth in the images they created. The realism that is characteristic of Renaissance artwork is a dramatic contrast to the flat, one-dimensional paintings produced in Medieval times. **(C)** Medieval paintings were not very realistic. **(D)** The museum currently has an exhibit about Russian sculptors. Whether of the Medieval or the Renaissance period, all artists can learn from the attempts and the accomplishments of those who preceded them.

---

8. **(A)** Our dog is not used to having such a big fenced yard in which to run and play. The first day at my new school was not the disaster that I had feared and expected. **(B)** As soon as I reached the school grounds, a nice girl introduced herself and offered to give me a quick tour of the school. I accepted since my dad dropped me off early to become familiar with the school. **(C)** The girl's name was Marnie. I was thankful that I was not alone as I walked into the school's main building for the very first time. As we strolled to my homeroom, Marnie was thoughtful enough to introduce me to a few of her friends. **(D)** After a pleasant start to my first day, I was excited to meet my teachers and get my books.

9. When construction of a new building began a block from where we live, we had no idea how much of an inconvenience it would truly be. We were miserable for two long months. **(A)** For the first two weeks, the constant roaring and crashing of the bulldozers as they cleared the ground went on well into the evening. That noise does not account for the other heavy equipment they used. **(B)** The grocery store does not have the cereal I prefer. I was almost relieved when the workers started hammering together the frame of the building. **(C)** Soon, though, the constant striking and pounding of metal against metal became even more annoying than the heavy equipment! **(D)** After the construction was done, it took weeks before the awful noises got out of our heads.

---

10. **(A)** Our neighbors and my family went to a nearby amusement park last weekend. We all had a wonderful time, especially because the weather was so nice. Our neighbor John kept trying to win stuffed animals. **(B)** Finally, on his last turn, he knocked enough bottles down to win a giant gray dolphin. I played some of the sports games, including the baseball toss and the basketball free-throw game. After a lot of fast rides, we took a break and enjoyed a spin on the Ferris wheel. **(C)** We liked the Ferris wheel, but most of us liked the thrill of the roller coasters better. For lunch, we got our coolers, unpacked their contents, and ate sandwiches, fruit, and pretzels. **(D)** The pool will open next week.

---

11. My brother wrote a story for me about the Mojave Desert. Did you know it is in California? My brother knows I love animals so he based the story on a desert iguana named Momo. **(A)** The story tells how Momo only comes out as the sun sets in the desert because it is so warm. **(B)** Momo spends a lot of time trying to find a source of water for a cool, refreshing drink. When he finds a particular type of cactus, Momo can carefully snip open one of its hearty leaves for a sip of water. **(C)** Many plants have hidden means of protection. **(D)** Momo is not the only desert creature in the story. Momo's pal is a kangaroo rat named Gilly. They play tic-tac-toe with their tails.

Unit 2

Narrative Paragraphs

While it is important to stay on topic in a paragraph, it is also important to avoid repetition and wordiness. **Repetition** is writing the same or a similar word or thought over and over again. **Wordiness** refers to using too many words to express an idea. Both of these things can cause a reader to lose interest. Even if it is not narrative, an effective paragraph contains words and sentences that are clear and specific. It also includes a variety of words. Do not be afraid to use different words or new vocabulary as long as you use them correctly.

Read each paragraph pair to decide which paragraph is more interesting because it is clear and *not* repetitive.

12. **(A)** My grandparents grow jasmine. There are two hundred known jasmine species that are native to tropical and subtropical regions of the world. Many jasmine varieties are shrubs that produce white, pink, or yellow flowers. Because of the jasmine flower's delicate scent, its oil is used in perfumes and scented lotions. Jasmine is also used to flavor hot tea.

    (B) I know people who grow jasmine. There are so many species of jasmine. Jasmine originally grows in tropical and subtropical regions of the world. Many jasmine species are shrubs. These shrubs produce white blossoms. They also produce pink or yellow blossoms. Because of the flower's delicate flower scent, the flower's oil is used in perfumes. The oil is also used in scented lotions. Jasmine tea, which can be served hot, is flavored with jasmine.

---

13. **(A)** As we reached the edge of the river, we saw a small boat bobbing in the water on the other side of the river. The bobbing boat was tied with a long rope to a dock that was rundown. Supplies were piled inside the boat, as if its owner had prepared for a long journey. Apparently guarding the boat, a dog rested on the dock near the boat.

    (B) As we reached the edge of the river, we saw a small boat bobbing upon the water on the opposite bank. The boat was tied to a rundown dock with a long rope. Piled inside the watercraft, supplies had been prepared for the assumed owner's long journey. Apparently guarding the boat, a dog rested and waited for its owner.

Unit 2
Narrative Paragraphs

14. (A) *The Black Stallion* is a fictional story about a close bond between a boy and a wild horse. During a shipwreck, the wild horse pulls Alec to safety, and the wild horse is freed by Alec. Alec begins to rely on the wild horse, and the wild horse begins to rely on Alec. The wild, black horse comes to trust Alec, and soon Alec rides the horse. Alec and the horse are saved. A race filled with excitement awaits Alec and the black stallion.

(B) *The Black Stallion* is a fictional story about a close bond between a boy named Alec and a wild horse. During a shipwreck, the stallion that Alec freed from a stall pulls Alec to safety onto a deserted island. The two begin to rely on each other for survival. Soon, the magnificent black stallion trusts Alec enough to be ridden. After their rescue, Alec rides the stallion in a race filled with excitement.

---

15. (A) My new aquarium has many exotic fish. At the top of the tank, three zebra danios dart back and forth in a chase. A school of large silver and black tetras slowly patrol the area around the zebra danios. Toward the front of the tank, twenty multicolored neon tetras cluster together behind a water plant. Three catfish hover along the bottom of the tank and hide among the rocks.

(B) My new aquarium has many fish, and many of the fish are exotic. Three really exotic zebra fish chase each other. Some other fish, which are big, black, and silver, hang out around those zebra fish. Then, at the front of the tank, a bunch of bright, neon fish that are many, many colors hide close together by some plant. These other fish hide closer to rocks on the tank's floor, almost at the very bottom.

---

16. (A) Two months ago, I began training for a five-mile marathon. On my first day of training, I could not run half a mile without stopping for a rest. As days continued, I ran even farther without stopping. Gradually, my form improved, and my distance increased. Training was worthwhile, as I easily finished the marathon.

(B) Two months ago, I began training for this marathon, which is at least a few miles long. I could not run that far at all without stopping on my first day of running. As days went on, I could run more and more without a stop to rest. Soon enough I was running farther and farther in an improved way. Training was good, and I did the marathon easily.

Unit 3
Narrative Paragraphs

Dialogue

Dialogue is the words that are spoken by characters in a real or make-believe story. Dialogue is often used in narrative paragraphs. Some tips for writing dialogue include the following:

- Use quotation marks to set off the speaker's words, and use a speaker tag before or after the quotation to identify the speaker.

  "Alice, it's time for bed," Mom said gently.

- Begin a new paragraph each time a different person speaks.
- Dialogue should sound like what a person would normally say. Also, each new line of dialogue should make sense based on what was said just before it.

Which new line of dialogue makes the most sense based on what was said just before it?

1. It was another Saturday morning, which is when my sister and I are supposed to clean our room. I began to place books back on their shelves while my sister sat at her desk reading a magazine. As I finished that task, she still sat there ten minutes later, and I was really getting annoyed.

   "Sarah," I said firmly, "it is your room too, so get out of that chair and please help me clean it up!"

   ______

   (A) "Are you girls almost ready for lunch?" Dad yelled from downstairs in the kitchen.

   (B) "Hold on a minute," said Sarah. "I will help you clean our room as soon as I read just one more article."

   (C) "Do you want to combine our allowances to buy Ethan's birthday present?" asked Sarah. Ethan is our brother.

2. The first of many bands left the stage. When the audience started to quiet down, the master of ceremonies walked across the stage and picked up the microphone. I recognized his voice because he is a disc jockey on a local radio station that I listen to a lot.

   "Ladies and gentlemen, there is a very special guest I would like to introduce you to tonight," he announced.

   ______

   (A) "Please give another round of applause for that performance."

   (B) "Please welcome our special guest, the very talented Tony Bates."

   (C) "The first portion of our show tonight will be several songs performed by a local group of rising stars."

3. The doorbell rang, and Mom went to see who was there. Three girls dressed in scouting uniforms stood on the steps. One of the girls held a clipboard and a pencil.

______

"I do not have enough cash to buy a calendar right now," Mom explained.

(A) "Do you have any yard work I could do?" asked a neighbor's son.
(B) "Do you have any daughters?" asked the girl in the middle.
(C) "Would you like to buy a calendar to help our organization?" asked one of the other girls.

---

4. Paul and André rushed to the playground's basketball court. Suddenly, Paul stopped to pick up something off the ground.

"What did you find?" asked André.

"It is a twenty dollar bill!" said Paul excitedly.

______

"I will keep the money only if no one reports it lost," answered Paul.

(A) "Are you going to keep it?" asked André.
(B) "We have to wait for the basketball court again," said André.
(C) "I am glad we are friends," said André.

---

5. Last week, my brother and I rode our bikes to the library. We followed a bike path, which is nearly five miles there and back. About half way home, I felt a bump and heard my tire make a sighing sound.

"Your tire is going flat," my brother said.

______

I locked my bike to a post, and my brother and I took turns riding his bike home. We would return with my dad and his truck or a repair kit.

(A) "The bike path is only a few years old," my brother explained.
(B) "We'd better stop," I said.
(C) "Do you think it will rain?" I asked.

Which new line of dialogue makes the most sense based on what was said just before it?

6. The king's youngest son set off on a journey to seek his own future and fortune. Resting below the canopy of a tree in the forest, the king's son saw an old, old man with a full, white moustache that appeared to grow into his long, long beard.

____

Unlike his older brothers, the king's youngest son was kindhearted. He sat down beside the old man to share his supper and some stories.

(A) "Please sir," said the old man, "Can you spare any food for me? I have not eaten yet today."

(B) "How do you get to Harlow Falls?" asked the king's son.

(C) "Please sir," said the old man, "can you spare a blanket?"

---

7. Finally, the opening day of the movie my friends and I wanted to see has arrived. We asked for our parents' permission to go to this movie weeks ago! We have been saving our money to pay for the bus ride to the theater, the tickets to the movie, and refreshments. I called my friend Quinn to ask which day we should go.

____

I agreed with Quinn and asked her to call half of our friends who wanted to go to the movie. Then I would call the other half. We would write down when everyone could go, check the movie's schedule, and decide that way.

"Good plan," I replied. "Call me back when you are done with your part of calling our friends. Thank you for your help!"

(A) "How much money did you save?" asked Quinn.

(B) I asked my parents, "Do either of you know where the newspaper is?"

(C) "Before we decide on a day and a time," Quinn said, "we need to ask the others when they can go to the movie."

8. Lara is my cousin. My family and I went to visit Lara and her family soon after her birthday. One of her birthday gifts was a computer program that you can use to make your own greeting cards.

"Please show me a task that your new program can do," I requested.

______

"Wow! It really is fun to make greeting cards," I exclaimed.

(A) "How many cards have you made?" asked Lara's dad.

(B) "Would you like a snack?" asked my aunt.

(C) Lara said, "Here is one card I have already printed out. Watch the computer screen as I show you how it was designed."

---

9. The students waited in line. They were excited to sign up for the clubs that they wanted to participate in during the school year.

"Are you signing up for the photography club?" asked Keith.

"No, I did that last year," replied Ty. "I am signing up for the yearbook club this year."

______

(A) "My backpack does not have much in it," said Keith.

(B) "I was wondering because that is the club I would like to join," said Keith.

(C) "Who is going to the dance with you next Saturday?" asked Keith.

---

10. Have you ever heard of zoo detectives? When the zoo is closed, Egbert the elephant and Rufus the rhinoceros solve mysteries at the zoo, such as stolen bananas or unlocked gates. Currently, they are working together to find out how one of the owls gets out at night.

While looking for clues, Rufus asked Egbert, "Where does the owl go?"

______

(A) "The owl perches upon a bench in the courtyard," replied Egbert.

(B) "I think I hear a raccoon behind that building," said Egbert.

(C) "Do you wish you had a trunk like mine?" Egbert asked.

Unit 4
Narrative Paragraphs

Closing Sentences

Once you have a topic sentence and supporting sentences or details in your narrative paragraph, it is necessary to write a related closing sentence. A **closing sentence** sums up the main idea of a paragraph. It can provide a final thought about the paragraph or serve as a transition to the next paragraph on the same topic. A closing sentence is the last sentence of a paragraph.

Which closing sentence best completes each narrative paragraph?

1. Mary Leakey was an archaeologist who made many discoveries throughout her career. She uncovered and interpreted more than one thousand prehistoric cave paintings in Africa. She also traced the development of Stone Age tools. Mary Leakey discovered an animal skeleton that dated back over sixteen million years; it revealed a link between monkeys and apes. She also found a human-like skull that was nearly two billion years old! Fossilized footprints Leakey discovered suggested that creatures walked upright more than three billion years ago. _____

   (A) With discoveries like those of Leakey's, we can all learn important things about our planet's history.
   (B) Archaeology is the scientific study of past materials and life forms.
   (C) Three billion years is an amount of time I cannot imagine.

2. The Pony Express was a mail delivery service that operated in 1860 and 1861. It was formed because it took three weeks for mail to be delivered by stagecoach from St. Joseph, Missouri, to Sacramento, California. During that time period, those who had gone to California to find gold wanted a faster way to communicate with their families in the East. With 190 stations between St. Joseph and Sacramento, riders of the Pony Express transported mail in ten days or less. _____

   (A) Immediate communication is necessary in a time of emergency.
   (B) The Pony Express was no longer needed once the telegraph was introduced in 1861.
   (C) Horses pulled stagecoaches.

3. A twelfth-century painting was stolen from the museum. The museum's curator surveyed the scene. She immediately recognized a notorious art thief's calling card, a silver glove. From wherever this thief stole, he or she left one silver glove in place of the stolen item or artwork. The thief is thought to be a woman due to the glove's size, but the thief could be a man using a woman's glove to confuse investigators. A similar glove was left behind when the Lala Opal was stolen from a Spanish museum. The museum's curator called the local police and the detective who worked on the opal case. _____

(A) Together, they hope to capture the thief and retrieve the treasures that have been lost.

(B) A curator is a person who oversees and cares for something.

(C) More than one color can be seen when you look into most opals.

---

4. Every few years, my family and I travel to the Grand Canyon in Arizona. It is always breathtaking, especially since we notice something new each time. We have been fortunate enough to camp both away from and near the Colorado River, which runs at the base of the Grand Canyon. It is actually the river that has carved much of the canyon's formation. Horizontal layers of canyon rock vary from red to brown. When the sun rises or sets, color fills the canyon. _____

(A) Though there is plenty to describe, nothing is as stunning as seeing the Grand Canyon for yourself.

(B) Camping is tiring, but fun.

(C) Some Grand Canyon rocks are more than a billion years old.

---

5. My first experience acting in a play was awful. I had never been comfortable speaking in front of an audience, but one of my friends convinced me that trying it would be fun. Instead of a minor role that would not require much talking, I was chosen for one of the lead roles. My friend, who talked me into participating in the play, accepted a lead role also. I had so many lines that it was difficult to remember them. On the play's opening night, I tripped on the stage's curtain while making my first entrance. _____

(A) I would like to see an opera performed live.

(B) My brother is on the football team with a friend of mine.

(C) Luckily, with a friend's support, the rest of the play went well.

The First LAP
Language Activity Pages

A. Exercising Your Skill

You have been learning about paragraph structure, with a focus on narrative writing. You have learned about topic sentences, staying on topic, dialogue, and closing sentences. Number your paper from 1 to 10. Read each sentence below to decide if it is true or false. If the sentence is true, write the letter **T** on your paper. If it is false, write **F.**

1. Sentences in a paragraph do not have to be related.
2. A paragraph should tell about a specific topic.
3. Mainly, narrative writing tells all or part of a story.
4. A topic sentence can occur at the beginning of a paragraph.
5. A topic sentence can occur at the end of a paragraph.
6. Topic sentences should not share the main idea of a paragraph.
7. Staying on topic is not important when writing a paragraph.
8. Dialogue is not used in make-believe stories.
9. Dialogue refers to the words spoken by story characters.
10. A closing sentence is the last sentence of a paragraph.

B. Expanding Your Skill

Number your paper from 1 to 5. Although written incorrectly, some of the lines below are dialogue. On your paper, write the letter of each line that needs to be corrected.

(A) Dad asked Rena and Max to go to the store. (B) Dad ran out of some ingredients to finish Mom's special anniversary dinner. (C) They were more than happy to help.

(D) I need brown sugar, corn starch, vanilla, and flour, said Dad.

(E) Rena asked, Will these items be in the same aisle of the store?

(F) Dad replied, I think so. They should be where the baking goods are.

(G) Rena and Max were getting their coats on when Dad came rushing toward them. (H) I am so glad I caught you both in time. I also need fresh flowers, said Dad. I am going to decorate Mom's cake with them.

(I) Sure thing, said Max, We will get the prettiest flowers we see.

C. Exploring Language

Narrative Writing Number your paper from 1 to 5. Read the make-believe story below to answer the questions that follow.

Cars are extraordinary things. Not long ago, there was an extraordinary car that could see, talk, feel, and process information. The car's name was Mika. <u>If something was wrong with Mika, you could ask what was wrong, and Mika could tell you.</u> Whoever got to drive Mika never had to worry about having an accident, locking his or her keys in the car, forgetting to shut off the lights, or installing an alarm. Mika could help with all of these things. **I wonder what age you have to be to drive in Europe.** Mika was the only car of its kind and eventually was put in a museum. Mika hoped to be used as a resource from which others could learn.

1. Which of these sentences is the paragraph's topic sentence?
   (A) Mika could help with all of these things.
   (B) Not long ago, there was an extraordinary car that could see, talk, feel, and process information.
2. Does the underlined sentence stay on topic?
   (A) Yes **(B)** No
3. Does the boldfaced sentence stay on topic?
   (A) Yes **(B)** No
4. Is there an example of dialogue in this paragraph?
   (A) Yes **(B)** No
5. Which of these sentences is the paragraph's closing sentence?
   (A) Mika hoped to be used as a resource from which others could learn.
   (B) Mika was the only car of its kind and eventually was put in a museum.

D. Expressing Yourself

Choose one of these activities. When you are finished, give your paper to your teacher.

1. Select a topic for a brief narrative paragraph. Then write your paragraph. Make sure your topic sentence, supporting details, and closing sentence are clear and related. If relevant, use dialogue.
2. **WORK with a PARTNER** Find a partner. Together, write a narrative paragraph that tells a make-believe story. Follow the guidelines above, but this time dialogue is required. Name the characters and places you create.

Unit 5
Persuasive Paragraphs

Topic Sentences

Another type of paragraph is the **persuasive paragraph.** Its purpose is to convince readers to think, feel, or act a certain way. Many times a persuasive paragraph's writer attempts to get readers to agree with his or her opinion.

In a persuasive paragraph, a topic sentence is important because it can clarify a writer's goals or highlight an opinion. A persuasive paragraph's topic sentence can help focus the reader on a particular viewpoint. As long as it makes sense, a topic sentence can be anywhere in a paragraph. In persuasive writing, a topic sentence is typically at the beginning.

Which topic sentence best completes each persuasive paragraph?

1. _____ Many Japanese people continue to live actively and productively well into their eighties. Much of this is due to what they consume. Miso, a fermented soy liquid, is unique to the Japanese diet. Studies have shown miso to be effective in preventing certain types of cancer and high cholesterol. Green tea, another Japanese staple, also helps to prevent some cancers, high blood pressure, and heart disease.
   (A) Japan is one of the most industrialized countries in the world.
   (B) In Japan, elderly people are treated with great respect.
   (C) A traditional Japanese diet provides benefits not found in the diets of other countries.

2. A dog is always excited to see its owner. A dog is a great companion that is eager to play or go for a walk. On the other hand, if a dog's owner is not feeling well or would prefer to read, a dog rests quietly nearby. Most dogs can be trained to perform useful tasks, such as fetching things or opening doors. Dogs are usually more outgoing than cats, and many dogs actually get along with cats. Some dogs will risk their lives to protect their owners from harm. _____
   (A) These are reasons why I think a dog is a better pet than a cat.
   (B) Dogs are animals.
   (C) Sometimes a dog barks when there is no threat of danger.

3. Everyone who knows how to write a letter should consider having a pen pal. If you have a pen pal in a different country, he or she can teach you about his or her culture, such as customs, food, history, and celebrations. You can explain your culture as well. A pen pal can become a trustworthy friend with whom you share your thoughts and feelings. Also, if you ever visit the country where your pen pal lives, he or she just might show you around! Talk to a librarian today about the resources available to find a pen pal. _____

(A) Having a pen pal is one of the most worthwhile hobbies a person can have.

(B) The library I go to does not have extended hours on weekends.

(C) Last year my family planned a trip to Europe, but our passport paperwork was lost in the mail.

---

4. _____ First of all, Clark has experience because he was a student council member last year. Clark gets along well with others and has gotten to know almost all of the students at school. As well as being a good speaker, Clark listens with care and expresses himself clearly. He has even offered to take a student survey of their concerns. Clark also possesses leadership qualities, as he has acted as debate team vice president for two years. Cast your vote for Clark for student council president today!

(A) Clark really wants to be a member of student council.

(B) Clark leads the soccer team with the most assists, and he is the team's cocaptain.

(C) Clark is a qualified candidate for student council president.

---

5. _____ The Everglades of Florida help to control flooding. They provide a supply of clean water to many Florida residents. The Everglades are home to many species of plants and animals that do not exist anywhere else in the world. Thus they provide shelter for a variety of wildlife and support food chains. In addition, the Everglades are an important source of revenue because of tourism.

(A) There are numerous colleges and universities throughout Florida.

(B) The Everglades are an essential natural habitat, especially to the state of Florida, that should be protected.

(C) Florida is a peninsula.

Unit 6

Persuasive Paragraphs

Order of Arguments

A persuasive paragraph makes a claim and supports the claim with arguments, or evidence. A **claim** is a position or viewpoint that the writer must prove by the use of arguments. An **argument** is a reason for or against an idea.

Claim: A democracy is the best form of government.

Argument That Supports the Claim: In a democracy, people are free to choose their leaders.

- A persuasive paragraph often includes several arguments to support the claim. These arguments can be organized from weakest to strongest so the last point leaves a lasting impression on the reader. Another strategy is to organize arguments from strongest to weakest so the most important argument grabs the reader's attention.

The arguments in each paragraph below are organized from weakest to strongest. Choose the argument that fits the claim and best completes each paragraph.

1. The amount of time that children and young adults spend playing video games should be limited. _____ Constantly playing video games also takes time away from being outdoors or from spending quality time with family. Worst of all, children and young adults who are obsessed with video games may actually suffer health problems as a result of poor eating habits and inactivity.
   (A) Chores do not get done when too many video games are played.
   (B) Playing video games only takes a small amount of time away from doing homework, which can be finished later when the game is over.
   (C) Video games offer an exciting and much-needed daily break.

2. We should have a math club at school. _____ A math club could sponsor fun activities to get more students interested in math. Most importantly, students who join the math club could meet to enrich their math skills and make new friends at the same time.
   (A) Twenty students just joined the science club.
   (B) Math and English are two very different subjects.
   (C) Our school needs more academic clubs.

3. Have you ever tried to write a report without planning it first? A report should always be planned. _____ Another good reason to plan is that it helps you decide what kind of information you need, where to get it, and how to organize it once you find it. If your report needs to be in time order, planning will help you place events exactly where they happened. If your report has a word limit, planning it first will help you avoid having too little or too much to say. Planning helps you avoid errors because you have thought out what you want to say.

(A) You should always proofread your report when you have finished revising it.

(B) When you plan, you have a schedule to follow so you feel less anxious about finishing your report on time.

(C) A research report should always include at least three paragraphs.

---

4. You should donate clothes, games, toys, and books that you no longer use or want to the school's yard sale. _____ If you have outgrown some of your clothes or toys, donate them. If you have clothes you never wear or games you never play, donate them. If you have books you do not read anymore, donate them. The money that is raised from the sale will be used to buy supplies for or make repairs on the school. School fees may even be lowered. Students and employees of the school will benefit from the yard sale, so we all should help make it a success.

(A) There are so many different charities and organizations that need people's support.

(B) Small or large, any donation should make you feel good because you contributed.

(C) My homeroom teacher, Ms. Eskrise, will be supervising the yard sale this year.

Unit 6
Persuasive Paragraphs

The arguments in each paragraph below are organized from strongest to weakest. Choose the argument that fits the claim and best completes each paragraph.

5. I think it is a good idea for schools to have a dress policy that requires students to wear uniforms. _____ Also, parents would save money because they would not have to buy as many items of clothing for their children. Students would save time, too, because they would not have to go shopping constantly for the latest clothing and fashion accessories. Their morning routines would be shorter because they would not have to spend time choosing an outfit to wear. The proposed dress policy would make life a lot easier for students, teachers, and parents.

(A) Time and time again schools have tried to enforce dress policies, but they have never been entirely successful.

(B) Aren't students' rights trampled on when they are forced to wear school uniforms?

(C) Students spend so much time worrying about how they look and how others look that they are distracted from learning, which is the whole point of going to school.

6. Recycling is a great way to show you care about our planet and its future generations. _____ Less waste equals less pollution and a cleaner way of life. If you recycle, you can get rid of things that you do not want in your home. Recycling means that the garbage cans or bags you have to move or carry outside will not be as heavy as they used to be. When you recycle, you usually get a special recycling bin to place on the curb for pickup.

(A) Recycling empowers us to reduce the planet's waste and reuse many materials to save vital resources.

(B) Newspapers and plastics are usually placed in separate recycling bins.

(C) Some people feel that recycling is not worth their time and effort, and they may be right.

7. The name of the gifted and talented program at our school should be changed. _____ For example, some students in our school have won awards for their artwork or trophies for their athletic abilities, but they are not in the gifted and talented program. There is nothing wrong with having special classes for students who get good grades and want to learn more about a subject, but to be fair our school should change the name of the gifted and talented program to the "learning enrichment" program. That way, the people who are in the program would not be seen as better than the other students, and every student in our school could feel free to think of himself or herself as gifted or talented in some way.

(A) After all, our gifted and talented program is one of the best in the country.

(B) The name of the program really isn't important.

(C) Calling only a small group of fifteen students in each grade "gifted" and "talented" makes it seem like the rest of the 326 students in our school do not have any gifts or talents, which is far from the truth.

---

8. Yesterday, another beautiful, perfectly healthy tree was cut down in my neighbor's front yard for no good reason. This needless destruction of trees is taking place all over our community, and it has to stop. _____ Trees also add beauty to our landscape. Without trees, all we would see when we looked out the window would be grass and buildings. There would be no trees to provide shade on sunny summer days. So, to preserve the beauty and overall health of our environment, speak up and encourage your neighbors to stop destroying trees.

(A) Trees are an important part of our ecosystem because they provide much needed shelter to wildlife and they produce oxygen, which helps keep the air we breathe pure and clean.

(B) There are many types of trees, including elm, beech, maple, oak, and sycamore.

(C) After a tree is cut down, it is a good idea to remove the stump.

Unit 6
Persuasive Paragraphs

Fact and Opinion

As you support your claim in a persuasive paragraph, you will notice that some of your evidence is **fact** and some is **opinion.** Facts are true and can be proved with research. Opinions are not always true and reflect a person's thoughts or feelings. It is important to understand this difference since the goal of persuasive writing is to convince readers to think, feel, or act a certain way or to agree with a specific viewpoint.

Fact: All trees do not produce the same type of leaf.

Opinion: The Douglas fir is my favorite tree.

For persuasive writing in general, do your best to support your claim with facts. When necessary, research your claim to gather factual evidence. However, opinions made by experts can be helpful also.

Which fact or opinion best supports each claim? If neither piece of evidence supports the claim, choose *Neither*.

9. **Claim:** Reading or watching something scary before going to sleep will give a person nightmares.
   Evidence: My brother and I both have bad dreams after our older sister reads our favorite scary poem to us.
   Evidence: _____
   (A) My sister is in high school, and sometimes we do our homework at the same time.
   (B) I do not watch many scary movies, and my brother does not watch many funny movies.
   (C) Neither

---

10. **Claim:** Traveling on back roads is more dangerous than traveling on highways.
    Evidence: Highways have plenty of lighting and are always paved.

    Evidence: _____
    (A) Most back roads have fewer travelers, so drivers tend to operate their vehicles more recklessly.
    (B) Motorcycles should not be ridden when roads are slick or snow-covered.
    (C) Neither

11. **Claim:** I study better and get more homework done in a quiet place, such as a library.

Evidence: Some studies have revealed that many people are able to focus better in an environment that has little or no noise.

Evidence: _____

(A) When there is less disruption or distraction, I read more accurately and do not read lines over and over again.

(B) The library we have at school is going to be expanded.

(C) Neither

---

12. **Claim:** Eyeglasses are easier to damage than contact lenses.

Evidence: Putting eyeglasses on and taking eyeglasses off can stretch the frames or scratch the lenses.

Evidence: _____

(A) No one in my family needs or wears eyeglasses or contact lenses.

(B) Contact lenses are not handled as frequently as eyeglasses.

(C) Neither

---

13. **Claim:** Penguins cannot fly.

Evidence: The wings or flippers of a penguin enable penguins to swim quickly and steer precisely while in the water.

Evidence: _____

(A) Some male penguin species take turns with the mother in caring for and guarding their baby penguins.

(B) A penguin's body weighs too much for a penguin to use its flippers to lift itself off the ground.

(C) Neither

---

14. **Claim:** Newspapers are a wonderful source when researching current events around the world.

Evidence: A majority of newspapers are printed on a daily basis.

Evidence: _____

(A) If you are holding and flipping through a newspaper, be careful not to get its ink all over your fingers and hands.

(B) I had a newspaper route when I was ten; it was my very first job.

(C) Neither

Unit 7
Persuasive Paragraphs

Closing Sentences

As with other paragraphs, it is necessary to have a closing sentence once your persuasive paragraph's topic sentence and evidence that supports its claim are written. Remember that a closing sentence sums up the main idea of a paragraph or serves as a transition to the next paragraph. In persuasive writing, the closing sentence can be another chance to state or reinforce your claim. Closing sentences occur last in a paragraph.

Which closing sentence best completes each persuasive paragraph?

1. More than three hundred years after his death, Galileo remains one of the greatest scientists who ever lived. His greatness stemmed from curiosity, which led to the creation of many useful devices. Galileo's best-known invention is the telescope, an amazing triumph for his era. Over a period of several years, Galileo used his telescope to make many new discoveries. His discoveries include the phases of Venus, sunspots, craters on the moon, and the moons of Jupiter. Another scientific success is the microscope Galileo is credited for inventing. He used it to study small objects during the daytime. ____

   (A) Galileo was born in 1564 and died in 1642.
   (B) These are only some of the reasons why Galileo is one of the greatest scientists ever.
   (C) Galileo's scientific focuses were astronomy and physics.

---

2. If you want to send a card to someone for a special occasion, why not design your own card on a computer? I think it is better than buying a card because you can personalize the message. Another nice feature of making a card on a computer is experimenting with font styles, sizes, and colors. You can decide what looks best. Designing a card allows you to insert original drawings or computer clip art. Borders and shading can also be added for that special someone. The best part of making a card is the thought that went into it. ____

   (A) There is no better card to remember someone with than a one-of-a-kind card.
   (B) Many greeting cards from stores are overpriced.
   (C) There is a variety of computer programs for all types of original projects.

3. The expression "That's like comparing apples and oranges" may sound okay, but it is misleading. Why do people use it when they mean that two things cannot be compared? Though apples and oranges are different, they can still be compared and do share similarities. Both are fruit, both have a round shape, and both can have seeds and be peeled. The expression should be changed to include two things that cannot be compared because they have nothing in common, for example, dirt and pillows. _____

(A) Oranges are usually more of a mess to eat than apples.
(B) Apples and oranges are commonly used in salads and baking.
(C) If it matters how an expression sounds, then it should also matter whether or not the expression makes sense.

---

4. Volunteering is a rewarding way to spend your free time. Not only do you get to choose where you would like to volunteer, you get to help people, animals, buildings, or the environment. As you meet other volunteers, there is a really good chance you will make some new friends. That is because you and the other volunteers probably have similar interests, since you are volunteering at the same place. As a volunteer, you might even get to be outside and see new places. _____

(A) My family volunteered together at an animal shelter.
(B) Volunteering is terrific for those you help and for you!
(C) You have to budget your time well if you become a volunteer.

---

5. We attended an outdoor concert at a venue we had been to before. We had much better seats this time than the last time. The concert stage was only seven rows away. On stage, instruments were set up in a crescent shape. We could see the performers clearly; nothing blocked our view. Last time, giant speakers kept us from seeing the stage. Speakers of varied sizes were stacked on the sides of the stage. Also, these seats were better because you could hear more music and less audience chatter. Even the seats themselves were more comfortable since they were larger than our previous seats and had padded armrests. _____

(A) The musicians must be exhausted from their hectic schedule.
(B) I had never seen speakers so huge.
(C) I would recommend the seats we had this time to anyone thinking about attending the same venue.

The Second LAP
Language Activity Pages

A. Exercising Your Skill

You have been learning more about paragraph structure, with a focus on persuasive writing. You have learned about topic sentences, the organization of arguments and evidence, the use of fact and opinion, and closing sentences. Number your paper from 1 to 10. Read each sentence below to decide if it is true or false. If the sentence is true, write the letter **T** on your paper. If the sentence is false, write the letter **F** on your paper.

1. The purpose of a persuasive paragraph is to convince readers to think, feel, or act however they want.
2. A topic sentence in a persuasive paragraph can be at the beginning of the paragraph only.
3. A topic sentence in a persuasive paragraph can help focus the reader on a particular viewpoint.
4. In persuasive writing, a claim is what you support.
5. Evidence is what you present to prove your claim.
6. Evidence is always presented from most to least important.
7. Facts can typically be backed up or proven with research.
8. Opinions are not always true.
9. In persuasive writing, it is better to support a claim with more opinions than facts.
10. A closing sentence cannot reinforce the claim of a persuasive paragraph.

B. Expanding Your Skill

Number your paper from 1 to 8. Read the persuasive paragraph below to decide if each numbered sentence is a fact or an opinion. On your paper, write **fact** if it is a fact or write **opinion** if it is an opinion.

(1) I think taking the bus to school is better than riding my bike or getting dropped off at school by my parents. (2) First of all, the bus is rarely late. (3) On the bus, I can read or spend time with my friends. (4) I also feel safer on the bus. (5) In addition, it is no fun to ride a bike when it is windy or rainy outside. (6) I often have too much to carry to school, so I cannot ride my bike. (7) There is usually not enough room to lock my bike to the school's bike rack. (8) Finally, sometimes my parents are behind schedule in the morning, so I would be late to school.

C. Exploring Language

Persuasive Writing Number your paper from 1 to 4. Read the persuasive paragraph below. Some of the evidence does *not* support the underlined topic sentence. Find the four pieces of incorrect evidence, and write the letter of each on your paper.

I do not think that reptiles should be kept as pets. (A) In their natural habitats, reptiles have as much room as they want to roam. (B) Unfortunately, most people cannot provide that kind of environment at home for a reptile. (C) A king cobra has a hood that appears when it feels threatened. (D) Reptiles have very specific eating habits, and many pet owners do not research the proper diet each reptile should have. (E) Some reptiles are thought to have prehistoric ancestors. (F) Since different reptiles thrive in various climates and habitats, it is too difficult for caretakers to re-create a reptile's original surroundings. (G) A Komodo dragon is the largest of all known lizards. (H) Komodo is the name of an Indonesian island. These are some reasons why reptiles should not be pets.

D. Expressing Yourself

Choose one of these activities. When you are finished, give your paper to your teacher.

1. Think of a topic, and write a brief persuasive paragraph. If needed, look back through the previous units to get ideas. Remember that you need to provide evidence to support your claim, and remember the difference between fact and opinion. Organize your paragraph's evidence from weakest to strongest or from least to most important. Make sure that your topic and closing sentences state and reinforce the same claim.

2. WORK with a PARTNER Find a partner. Select a topic together. Eventually it will be used for a brief persuasive paragraph. Separately, each of you should write four ideas you think or know about the topic. Then share and discuss those ideas with your partner. Decide which ideas you both agree upon because they will be the evidence in your paragraph. Together, before you write the paragraph, put the ideas or evidence in order from strongest to weakest or from most to least important.

Unit 8
Expository Paragraphs

Topic Sentences

A third type of paragraph is the **expository paragraph.** Its purpose is to explain how to do something or to present information. For example, an expository paragraph can summarize all or part of another piece of writing.

In an expository paragraph, a topic sentence is important because it states the main idea of what is being explained or addressed. As with other types of paragraphs, a topic sentence can occur in the beginning, middle, or end of the paragraph as long as it makes sense.

Which topic sentence best completes each expository paragraph?

1. Have you ever heard the debate over whether a tomato is a fruit or a vegetable? _____ A tomato develops from part of a flower, which puts it in the fruit category. On the other hand, a *true* fruit grows on woody, stemmed plants or trees. Therefore, the tomato can be classified as a vegetable because tomatoes grow on vines, not trees.

(A) Actually, a tomato is both a fruit and a vegetable.
(B) A tomato is used more like a vegetable than a fruit.
(C) A fresh, ripe tomato is actually my favorite summertime treat.

2. Do you know someone who has a racing bicycle, a tennis racket, or a golf club made with titanium? In addition to sports equipment, titanium is used for hip replacements and other artificial body parts. Wheelchairs used in sporting events, such as racing and basketball, are often made out of titanium. This valuable metal is essential to the automobile and aircraft industries. It is used to produce connecting rods, suspension springs, and airplane wings. _____

(A) Titanium is a metal obtained from the minerals *ilmenite* and *rutile*.
(B) Titanium's durability, strength, and light weight make it ideal for use in many products.
(C) Titanium weighs less than steel and iron.

3. _____ In China and Greece, red is the color of good luck. For Russians, red is a symbol of beauty. In South Africa, red is the color of mourning. In the United States, red serves as a symbol of warning.

(A) Red is one of the primary colors.
(B) Red is the most common color used in the flags of countries.
(C) The color red represents and means different things to people in various parts of the world.

---

4. _____ Body language refers to what a person's physical gestures communicate about his or her mood and feelings. Facial expressions refer to the face only and can also reveal a person's attitude. Shaking your head back and forth means "no" or expresses disagreement or disappointment. Putting an index finger up to your lips indicates that it is time to be quiet. Perhaps the ultimate body language is sign language, which is communicated with fingers, hands, and arms. As for facial expressions, who does not recognize that a smile expresses pleasure? People in all parts of the world also recognize that tense lips or a frown expresses displeasure. Raised eyebrows, wide eyes, and a slightly open mouth are easily recognized as a sign of shock or surprise.

(A) Though countless verbal languages are spoken throughout the world, some body language and facial expressions are well known.
(B) One person can have hundreds of facial expressions without ever seeing most of them.
(C) I wonder what it means to cross and fold your arms across your chest.

---

5. Would you enjoy a bit of tropical rain forest in your room year-round? If so, consider making a terrarium. _____ Start by getting an aquarium in a size you want. Cover the aquarium floor with half an inch of charcoal. Put a thin layer of loose, coarse soil over the charcoal. Choose your plants, and arrange them in the terrarium so their roots are covered with soil. Add rocks, wood scraps, shells, or other items to decorate the terrarium. Water the soil lightly. Then put a lid on the terrarium. Place your terrarium where plenty of sunlight will reach it.

(A) Terrariums do not need much care.
(B) A terrarium, which can house a variety of plants, is simple to make.
(C) A terrarium can be a home for certain small animals.

Unit 9

Expository Paragraphs

Facts and Details

Most of an expository paragraph consists of facts and details because something is being explained. Remember that facts are true and can be proved through research. Details include any additional information to support your topic. It is very important that all facts and details relate to the topic. If they do not, readers will get confused about the purpose of your paragraph.

Like other writing, an expository paragraph should be well organized. For example, when explaining a process or providing directions to a place, the steps should be organized in the order that they are to be completed. All information in an expository paragraph should be correct, complete, and clear.

Choose the fact or detail that does *not* belong in each expository paragraph.

1. **(A)** The Inuit are Native American people who settled in Canada about four thousand years ago. **(B)** The Inuit people were nomadic, which means that they moved from place to place rather than making a permanent home. **(C)** They traveled in large family groups, setting up camps and hunting animals that were native to that area. **(D)** The Great Lakes consist of five large lakes. **(E)** The Inuit faced the additional challenge of traveling over snow-covered terrain. **(F)** They overcame this snowy obstacle by using sleds pulled by dogs to transport their belongings. **(G)** When necessary, boats were used to move the Inuit's campsites across water.

2. **(A)** My sister has a subscription to her favorite magazine. **(B)** Recently, an interesting article appeared in many national newspapers. **(C)** The article explained that the United States Navy uses sea lions to protect some of its ships. **(D)** The sea lions swim safely alongside the ships to provide a warning if anything or anyone tries to approach the ships from below. **(E)** A navy spokesperson told reporters that sea lions were chosen because of their keen vision, even in dim light, and directional underwater hearing. **(F)** Sea lions also have the ability to dive up to six hundred and fifty feet below the water's surface.

3. **(A)** A checkerboard is a square game board that consists of sixty-four alternating red and black squares. **(B)** The game of checkers has to have two players. **(C)** On only the black squares of the outer three rows, each player places his or her twelve checker pieces, which look like thick plastic coins. **(D)** Checkers are moved diagonally onto one black square at a time, unless there is an opponent's checker to jump. **(E)** Players can jump only their opponent's checkers when the checker sits on a bordering square *and* the next square is without a checker. **(F)** Chess is played on the same type of game board though its colors vary. **(G)** The checker that is jumped is then removed from the board, taken by the jumper, and the game continues.

---

4. **(A)** A group of birds is not always called a *flock*. **(B)** Lions live in a *pride*. **(C)** For example, a group of geese on water is known as a *gaggle*. **(D)** A group of geese not flying in a v-formation is a *skein*. **(E)** A group of sparrows is called a *host,* while hawks or falcons assemble in a *cast*. **(F)** Hummingbirds form a *charm,* and quail convene in a *bevy* or a *covey*. **(G)** Owls join forces in a *parliament*. **(H)** A group of crows is known as a *muster* or a *murder*.

---

5. **(A)** Different maps present different information. **(B)** A topographical map shows an area's landforms, elevations, and bodies of water. **(C)** A person who draws maps is called a *cartographer*. **(D)** A demographic map shows an area's population distribution. **(E)** A road map shows an area's highways and streets. **(F)** A political map shows the boundaries between states, countries, and other territories. **(G)** A climatic map shows climate averages, including temperature and rainfall.

---

6. **(A)** Examine how a seed grows roots. **(B)** Choose a seed that sprouts quickly. **(C)** Fold a paper towel in fourths; moisten it with water. **(D)** Place the seed within the paper towel's folds. **(E)** We do not have room for a vegetable garden in our yard. **(F)** Put the paper towel inside a plastic bag, and then seal it. **(G)** The next day, open the bag, and unfold the towel to check the seed's roots. **(H)** Repeat this last step each day for a week; measure the length of the roots with a ruler.

Is the underlined fact or detail in the correct order in each expository paragraph?

7. Used as a gem, a pearl forms gradually within the body of an oyster. An oyster is a type of mollusk that lives in seas and oceans. An organ inside the oyster's shell, the mantle, produces a smooth, shimmering substance. This substance lines the inside of the oyster's shell. Oysters spend most of their time resting on beds of sand, so it is common for sand particles, or other tiny particles, to get inside the oyster's shell. The shimmering substance grabs and traps such particles. As the mantle continues to produce layers of the substance, it accumulates on the particle. Over time, the substance hardens into a pea-sized ball around the particle to form a pearl.

(A) Yes
(B) No

8. However, it is easy to learn how to use chopsticks. If you are not used to eating with chopsticks, they may feel clumsy or awkward at first. First, hold the upper chopstick in your hand like a pencil, about a third of the way from the top. Pointing in the same direction as the upper chopstick, place the lower chopstick against your ring finger and cradle it with your thumb. To pick up a piece of food, control the upper chopstick with your thumb and index finger while keeping the lower chopstick still.

(A) Yes
(B) No

9. From our school's parking lot, turn right onto Orchard Court. Heading toward the post office, continue north on Orchard Court for two miles. Turn right onto Connecticut Avenue. Stay on Connecticut Avenue for six blocks until you reach the intersection of Connecticut Avenue and Madison Road. Turn left onto Madison Road, and then turn right almost immediately at the next street. My house is the third one on the left. Here are the directions to get to my house for my party.

(A) Yes
(B) No

Unit 9
Expository Paragraphs

10. Would you like to send messages to a friend using invisible ink? More than likely, you already have everything you need to write a message in invisible ink. You need paper, milk, and a watercolor paintbrush. First pour some milk into a small bowl. Dip the tip of the thin paintbrush into the milk, and then write your message on an ordinary piece of paper. Use as little of the milk as you can, or else the paper will become too wet and wrinkled. Allow the milk to dry completely before giving the message to your friend. To read the message, your friend needs to hold the paper over a flashlight or a lightbulb. The heat of the light will cause the milk to turn brown, and the invisible message will appear.

(A) Yes
(B) No

---

11. If you like to eat fresh vegetables, you will love the edible vegetable bowl. First cut a green, red, or yellow pepper in half from stem to base, not across the middle. Trim off the pepper's stem, scoop out its seeds, and slice only one half of the pepper into thin strips. Next cut thin strips of celery, carrots, zucchini, cucumbers, or other vegetables you prefer. Place all of the vegetable strips inside the unused half of the pepper. You can add your favorite vegetable dip or salad dressing, mix, and enjoy!

(A) Yes
(B) No

---

12. It is easy to make miniature pizzas. Cut a bagel in half, and spread tomato sauce on both halves. If needed or desired, add seasonings such as basil and oregano to the sauce. Sprinkle shredded cheese of your choice over the sauce and seasonings. Add your favorite pizza toppings, including pepperoni, mushrooms, olives, and onions. Either in a toaster oven or a regular-sized oven, put the mini pizzas on a baking sheet lined with foil, and bake them until the cheese is melted. Open a small jar of tomato sauce. Enjoy your miniature pizzas alone, or share them with someone.

(A) Yes
(B) No

Unit 10

Expository Paragraphs

Closing Sentences

Once you have a topic sentence and the details of your expository paragraph have been explained, it is necessary to end with a related closing sentence. Remember that a closing sentence sums up the main idea of a paragraph or serves as a transition to the next paragraph. A closing sentence occurs last in an expository paragraph.

Which closing sentence best completes each expository paragraph?

1. A mature forest forms over a period of many years in a process called *succession*. The process begins in an open area of land with pioneer plant species, including grasses and small shrubs. At first, there is very little competition for sunlight. Small mammals, birds, worms, and insects gradually move into the area. As more plants grow and mature, however, the competition for sunlight increases. Taller plantlife, such as young trees, begins to block the sunlight from shorter plants. Many grasses and shrubs eventually die from a lack of sunlight, while the tallest plants and trees continue to thrive. _____

   (A) Forests provide shade while camping during hot weather.
   (B) A forest can be a relaxing or frightening place.
   (C) The process of succession continues in an endless cycle unless the forest is destroyed.

2. Have you ever heard the saying "Laughter is the best medicine"? Numerous medical studies have shown that laughter truly provides many health benefits. The act of laughing relaxes some of the upper body's muscles and reduces stress hormones. Laughter can also boost the body's immune system and internally massage the heart and lungs. Laughing increases the flow of oxygen, which stimulates the brain. Laughter is an all-around workout for the body, and may be why you feel exhausted after a long laugh. _____

   (A) The next funny joke you tell just might make someone really feel better!
   (B) Laughing can be disturbing, especially in a library.
   (C) I am not very good at telling jokes, but I like to tell stories.

3. To prepare a first-aid kit, get a sturdy, waterproof box with a lid that has several compartments. Pack the box with a pair of small scissors, tweezers, medical tape, an assortment of bandages, and a cold pack that can be activated. Be sure to include rubbing alcohol, antiseptic cream, gauze, cotton balls, aspirin, hydrogen peroxide, and a thermometer. A first-aid manual should be kept with the kit. _____

(A) In a medical emergency, never move the injured person.
(B) Write a list of emergency phone numbers to keep by the telephone.
(C) As you prepare the first-aid kit, make sure that all of the supplies fit, or increase the size of the box.

---

4. Recent surveys have shown that the drinking of milk is increasing among students. Experts credit the rise to four factors related to the packaging of milk. First, milk is now available in packages of different sizes that can be resealed. Second, milk is now available in a variety of flavors, such as strawberry or banana. Third, some schools supply milk in vending machines. Finally, improvements have been made to ensure that milk stays cold enough. _____

(A) I wonder if there will be any other milk flavors coming out soon.
(B) Milk is used in many recipes, such as sauces and desserts.
(C) It is hoped that the drinking of milk will continue to rise because milk provides essential vitamins.

---

5. Some animals have been known to show odd behaviors before an earthquake. For example, cats will often hide and not go outside. Dogs follow their owners from room to room, acting like something is wrong or barking constantly. Chickens fly to high perches and crowd together wildly. Mice and rats leap into the air, while pigs try to bite one another's tails. Although scientists cannot explain how these animals sense a pending earthquake, some scientists believe the animals can feel tiny vibrations that humans cannot. _____

(A) Precise instruments are used to predict and measure earthquake activity.
(B) Scientists also use their observations of such animals to help predict earthquakes.
(C) Certain locations are more at risk than others for earthquakes.

Unit 11
Writing Paragraphs

Descriptive Writing

Descriptive writing is the last type of writing introduced in this book. It is last because descriptive writing is often used in combination with other types of writing. For example, it is likely for a persuasive essay to have descriptive writing as part of its evidence to convince.

The purpose of a **descriptive paragraph** or descriptive writing is to provide the reader with a clear and vivid image of the writer's topic. This can include telling how the topic looks, feels, sounds, smells, and tastes, and sharing how the writer feels about the topic.

A description can be organized in many ways. The focus of this unit will be to organize a description from top to bottom. In other words, a topic is chosen and then described from its top to its bottom.

Based on the topic, does each paragraph have its description organized from top to bottom?

1. **Topic: Aloe Plants**

   An aloe plant grows in tropical areas and is known for its healing properties. The aloe's stalks are thickest at its base, and then they become thinner and narrow to a point. The aloe consists of numerous green stalks that curve upward from a central base. A clear gel fills the stalks, which makes them thick rather than flat. The gel is the part of the aloe that can heal. The stalks are covered with tiny jagged bumps.

   (A) Yes
   (B) No

2. **Topic: The Statue of Liberty**

   The Statue of Liberty is a one hundred and fifty-one-foot image of a woman. She faces the Atlantic Ocean, and one arm raises a torch high above her head. Upon Liberty's head is a simple crown that has seven spikes. Her gown is of classic Greek and Roman style. In her other, lowered hand, Liberty holds a tablet that reads "July 4, 1776" to signify United States independence. The statue, a gift from France, was completed in Paris in 1884 and stands on a huge pedestal.

   (A) Yes
   (B) No

3. Topic: Seahorses

Seahorses are unique creatures. To begin with, a seahorse is classified as a fish but looks nothing like one. The bodies of these unusual animals are covered with plates of prickly armor. Closer to its tail, a seahorse's dorsal fin moves it forward. Much like the shape of the letter *s,* a seahorse's body continues as its neck curves into its tail. Seahorses use their tails to hold onto things, such as kelp or seaweed. A seahorse probably got its name from how its head resembles that of a horse. At the top, a seahorse's head has an eye on both sides that moves independently and a long, thin snout. Small pectoral fins in the area of a seahorse's neck control its steering and turning.

(A) Yes
(B) No

---

4. Topic: Tarantulas

The tarantula is the largest spider in the world. It has eight hairy legs that can extend many inches from the sides of its main body segment. A tarantula often looks furry. Tarantulas have several beady black eyes and can have sharp fangs. Some tarantulas eat small reptiles and amphibians. Using specialized fangs, many tarantula species inject their prey with poison, thus paralyzing the prey. Tarantulas have round, segmented bodies covered with hair. A tarantula has two limb-like feelers near its head which are used to capture prey.

(A) Yes
(B) No

---

5. Topic: The Eiffel Tower

The Eiffel Tower in Paris is one of the most commonly recognized structures ever built. With an antenna, the top of the nine hundred and eighty-five-foot tower starts out thin. To assist in the climb, elevators function within part of the tower. This iron marvel widens as you continue down to its base. Of course, this is because the structure would not stand otherwise. The Eiffel Tower's base has four "feet," which create four broad and welcoming arches.

(A) Yes
(B) No

6. **Which paragraph would most likely be the descriptive part of an expository essay?**

(A) An albino is an animal that is white or atypically pale. An albino's body cannot produce pigment, which is responsible for giving an animal his or her color. As a result, most visible parts of an albino's body are white. For example, an albino squirrel will always be white instead of brown, gray, or black. However, the eyes of an albino appear pink because the animal's blood vessels are visible beneath the see-through irises. An iris is the part of an eye that gives it its color, such as hazel or green.

(B) Albinos are rare in nature, which is good because their unusual coloring easily attracts the attention of predators. A statistic reveals that about one in every twenty thousand animals is an albino. It is important to note that just because an animal has white fur does not necessarily mean that an animal is an albino.

7. **Which paragraph would most likely be the descriptive part of a persuasive essay?**

(A) Americans who live in the eastern part of the United States should plan to visit the West. From personal experience, I recommend driving instead of flying. You see so much more of the country and, I think, develop a greater appreciation of the United States' beauty. Do not forget to take your camera and its accessories because there are plenty of photo opportunities. Plan your journey out West today!

(B) In geographic terms, the eastern and western parts of the United States are quite different. Formations in the West are grand in scale, from the towering Rocky Mountains to the powerful Colorado River. Instead of pebbles scattered on river shores and in bare fields, there are massive rocks and boulders. Fortunately, the West does still have vast spaces without development, such as housing or shopping, for miles. Thousands of acres of forestland also occupy much of the West. The forests shelter animals seen only at zoos in the East.

8. Which paragraph would most likely be the descriptive part of a narrative essay?

(A) Nearly five thousand years ago, the Great Pyramid in Egypt was being built by thousands of workers. Altogether, the 2.3 million blocks of stone that make up the pyramid weigh approximately 6.5 million tons! Its measurements are mind-boggling. The Great Pyramid is triangular with a wide base and a pointed top. Time and wind have aged the pyramid.

(B) Large numbers must be used to describe the Great Pyramid of Egypt. About ten thousand workers spent twenty years building it. Considering their lack of technology, it is amazing the pyramid did not take one hundred years to build! For forty-three centuries, the Great Pyramid was the tallest structure on Earth.

---

9. Which paragraph would most likely be the descriptive part of an expository essay?

(A) Brazil's flag has a bright green background. Centered on the flag is a large yellow diamond with a blue sphere inside of it. Light in color, the blue sphere has very tiny stars on it. A banner that reads "Ordem E Progresso" arches across the middle of the sphere.

(B) In 1822, Brazil became independent. It is the largest country in South America. Its flag's motto translates to mean "order and progress." Brazil does not share any borders with Chile or Ecuador.

---

10. Which paragraph would most likely be the descriptive part of a persuasive essay?

(A) Space exploration can be a positive thing. Since space travel began in the 1960s, many important discoveries have been made, mostly about the moon. For example, the moon completes an orbit of Earth in twenty-seven days. An extraordinary event happened in 1969 when Neil Armstrong walked on the moon.

(B) Much of the moon's surface is flat. However, deep depressions called *craters* form on the moon when it is struck by comets and meteoroids. Similar to Earth, the moon has a crust, a mantle, and a solid core. Part of the moon's mantle is molten rock.

The Third LAP
Language Activity Pages

A. Exercising Your Skill

You have been learning more about types of paragraphs and their structure, with a focus on expository writing and a brief introduction to descriptive writing. You have reinforced the following skills: topic sentences, facts, details, closing sentences, and top-to-bottom organization of a description. Number your paper from 1 to 10. Read each sentence below to decide if it is true or false. If the sentence is true, write the letter **T** on your paper. If the sentence is false, write the letter **F** on your paper.

1. The purpose of an expository paragraph is to present information or to tell how to do something.
2. In an expository paragraph, a topic sentence can occur only at the beginning of the paragraph.
3. A topic sentence states the main idea of what is being explained in an expository paragraph.
4. Facts and details are common in expository paragraphs.
5. All information in an expository paragraph should be correct, complete, and clear.
6. When explaining a process, it does not matter how the steps are organized.
7. Closing sentences cannot serve as transitions to other paragraphs.
8. Descriptive writing should provide a vivid image for its reader.
9. A description can be organized from top to bottom only.
10. Descriptive writing is never used with other types of writing.

B. Expanding Your Skill

Number your paper from 1 to 5. Read each sentence below to decide if it is an example of a narrative, a persuasive, or an expository topic sentence. On your paper, write **N** for narrative, **P** for persuasive, or **E** for expository.

1. You should never leave a candle burning when no one is there.
2. Have you ever wondered how to grow soybeans?
3. Our ski trip lasted for five days, but it was cut short by a blizzard.
4. I think it is unfair that my brother gets his own room while I have to share one.
5. There are many steps to follow when making a piñata.

C. Exploring Language

Expository Writing Number your paper from 1 to 4. Read the paragraph below to answer the questions that follow.

The Panama Canal is a waterway through Panama that links the Atlantic Ocean to the Pacific Ocean. A treaty with Panama in 1903 gave the United States the permission to build and operate the canal. At that time, a ship leaving from New York City heading to San Francisco had to travel all the way around South America, a distance of over fifteen thousand miles. **When the canal was completed in 1914, a ship could make this journey in a distance of only six thousand miles.** In 1999, the United States and Panama signed a new treaty that gave Panama control of the canal. However, the United States can still defend the canal with military force if necessary. The Panama Canal has been beneficial for both sides.

1. Which of these sentences is the paragraph's topic sentence?
   (A) In 1999, the United States and Panama signed a new treaty that gave Panama control of the canal.
   (B) The Panama Canal is a waterway through Panama that links the Atlantic Ocean to the Pacific Ocean.
2. Does the underlined sentence support the paragraph's topic?
   (A) Yes **(B)** No
3. Is the boldfaced sentence in the correct order?
   (A) Yes **(B)** No
4. Are there any facts in this paragraph?
   (A) Yes **(B)** No

D. Expressing Yourself

Choose one of these activities. When you are finished, give your paper to your teacher.

1. Draw a simple map of how to get to school from where you live. Write an expository paragraph to provide step-by-step directions.
2. WORK with a PARTNER With a partner, think of a process to describe. Write an expository paragraph to explain the process in the correct order.

Unit 12

Writing Paragraphs

Figurative Language

Remember that the purpose of descriptive writing is to provide readers with a clear and vivid image of the topic. One way to accomplish this goal is to use **figurative language,** or figures of speech. Figurative language refers to words and expressions that create an image in a reader's mind without always keeping their true meanings. To achieve the planned and often dramatic effect of figurative language, it is important to use words that the reader will know and understand. Two common examples of figurative language are similes and metaphors.

- A **simile** uses the word *like* or *as* to compare two different things.
  The computer was buzzing like a hive of bees.
- A **metaphor** compares two different things without using *like* or *as*.
  The computer was a buzzing hive of bees.

Does each sentence include a simile or a metaphor?

1. A trail in the rain forest led us like a magic carpet.
   (A) Simile **(B)** Metaphor

2. The children marched in an orderly line as little soldiers.
   (A) Simile **(B)** Metaphor

3. The trend in bell-bottom jeans was a fire that was put out quickly.
   (A) Simile **(B)** Metaphor

4. My journal is a treasure chest that holds my precious memories.
   (A) Simile **(B)** Metaphor

5. Our neighbor's schedule is as regular as a clock.
   (A) Simile **(B)** Metaphor

6. Water is life; no living organism can exist without it.
   (A) Simile **(B)** Metaphor

7. The leaves floated downstream like tiny canoes.
   (A) Simile **(B)** Metaphor

Unit 12
Writing Paragraphs

Which word best completes each simile or metaphor?

8. Everyone treated me so well on my birthday that I felt like a ____.
   (A) sister **(B)** queen **(C)** daughter

9. My brother's eyes are as blue as the ____ on a clear day.
   (A) river **(B)** sun **(C)** sky

10. The ballerina was graceful like a ____.
    (A) dolphin **(B)** worm **(C)** gopher

11. Once we reached the top of the roller coaster's hill, my heart beat like a ____.
    (A) shoe **(B)** drum **(C)** door

12. The hailstones pounded upon the roof of the car like tiny ____.
    (A) buckets **(B)** fingers **(C)** hammers

13. The king was so broken-hearted that he cried a ____ of tears.
    (A) river **(B)** spoon **(C)** glass

14. Hawaii is a ____ unlike any place on Earth.
    (A) space **(B)** field **(C)** paradise

15. The lake is a ____ that reflects the bright moon.
    (A) stream **(B)** picture **(C)** mirror

16. With the windows closed on such a hot day, the room became an ____.
    (A) oven **(B)** igloo **(C)** egg

17. The stars were ____ sparkling in the velvety sky.
    (A) pins **(B)** gems **(C)** buttons

18. Reading is a ____ to knowledge.
    (A) tree **(B)** book **(C)** path

Unit 12
Writing Paragraphs

Another example of figurative language is **personification,** which compares ideas or objects as if they have human qualities.

My positive attitude does not hear your negativity.

The tree welcomed us with open arms.

Choose the words that complete each sentence and create an example of personification.

19. The laws of the United States ____ a person's age, race, and gender.
(A) ban discrimination against **(B)** do not see **(C)** protect

20. As it sank slowly into the horizon, the sun ____.
(A) changed color **(B)** set slowly **(C)** said good night

21. The canyon ____ us by sending back echoes of our voices.
(A) spoke to **(B)** repeated **(C)** did not surprise

22. The old house ____ during a severe storm.
(A) rattled **(B)** moaned **(C)** creaked

23. After the hurricane passed, the palm trees ____.
(A) dripped with water **(B)** were wet **(C)** drooped their heads

24. The breeze gently ____ petals from many flowers.
(A) blew **(B)** gathered **(C)** moved

25. The snowflakes ____ silently through the frosty air.
(A) dance **(B)** float **(C)** drift

26. This rule ____ be revised.
(A) should **(B)** was written to **(C)** is screaming to

27. The neglected car ____.
(A) is broken **(B)** needs to be fixed **(C)** refuses to start

Unit 12
Writing Paragraphs

One last example of figurative language is **exaggeration,** which stretches the truth. Sometimes exaggeration can add humor to writing, especially since it is written to emphasize a point and not the truth.

I know my house so well that I could get anywhere blindfolded.

Choose the sentence that includes an example of exaggeration.

28. **(A)** I have looked repeatedly to buy a new suitcase.
(B) I have looked everywhere to buy a new suitcase.
(C) I have looked at many stores to buy a new suitcase.

29. **(A)** That athlete's shoes are so big that I could use them as boats.
(B) That athlete's shoes are so big that he stumbled.
(C) That athlete's shoes are so big that my shoes look even smaller.

30. **(A)** My older brother is the best singer in the world.
(B) My older brother is the best singer in the room.
(C) My older brother is the best singer in our choir.

31. **(A)** The road is very long.
(B) The road becomes quite steep.
(C) The road continues forever.

32. **(A)** I would not like to give a speech.
(B) I will avoid giving a speech.
(C) I would rather do anything than give a speech.

33. **(A)** It was cold enough for my teeth to chatter.
(B) It was so cold that I froze.
(C) It was cold enough to see people's breath.

34. **(A)** You were so startled that you jumped right out of your skin.
(B) You were so startled that you screamed.
(C) You were so startled that you tripped over a rug.

35. **(A)** The ringing in my ears has lasted for a few minutes.
(B) The ringing in my ears is so loud.
(C) The ringing in my ears is killing me.

Unit 13
Writing Paragraphs

Word Choice

Word choice is important in all types of writing. If you take time to choose words carefully, your ideas will be clearer, and your writing will have a stronger impact on your readers.

- In a narrative paragraph, use strong action verbs and other descriptive words to show what characters are doing. When you write dialogue, choose words that fit each character's personality and do not seem out of place in the story.

  We walked along the beach. → We **strolled lazily** along the beach.

  "Mother, at what hour are we eating?" asked Jamal. → "Mom, when's dinner?" asked Jamal.

- In a persuasive paragraph, use words that will affect your audience the most. You can choose words that appeal to your readers' emotions or to their sense of reason.

  Your dog will be sad without a new Chew Town dog bone. (appeals to emotions)

  Chew Town dog bones reduce tartar buildup on dogs' teeth by 75%. (appeals to reason)

Choose descriptive words from the box to complete the narrative paragraphs below.

(A) glorious	**(B)** slays	**(C)** cautiously	**(D)** tormenting
(E) venture	**(F)** announces	**(G)** dreadful	

The story begins as Princess Una and the Red Cross Knight **1.** _____ **2.** _____ out to face the **3.** _____ dragon that has been **4.** _____ Una's kingdom. After many days of traveling, the knight sees a **5.** _____, shining palace on top of a mountain. The delighted knight **6.** _____, "Una and I should go there at once." However, an old hermit reminds him that he must ignore his own desires and face the dragon in the valley below.

After a lengthy, fierce battle, the knight overcomes all limitations and **7.** _____ the dragon. The king is so pleased that he changes the knight's name to Saint George of Merry England. The knight and Una are married, and they live happily ever after.

Unit 13
Writing Paragraphs

Answer each of the following questions about word choice in persuasive paragraphs.

8. Which sentence includes words that appeal to the readers' emotions?
   (A) If our community does not pass the tax levy, school budgets for sports will be decreased by 50% or more.
   (B) If our community does not pass the tax levy, children will suffer.
   (C) If our community does not pass the tax levy, the average class size will go up to thirty-five students.

---

9. Which sentence includes words that appeal to the readers' sense of reason?
   (A) One glass of Pure Juice contains the daily, doctor-recommended dose of vitamin C.
   (B) Drink Pure Juice so the oranges will not have given their lives in vain.
   (C) Drinking one glass of Pure Juice each day will make you feel like a new person.

---

10. Which sentence includes words that appeal to the readers' emotions?
    (A) Learn to play an instrument so you, too, can experience the joy of producing beautiful music for yourself and others.
    (B) Studies show that people who learn to play instruments actually increase their scores on math tests by 75%.
    (C) Learning to play an instrument can lower your blood pressure and help you think more clearly.

---

11. Which sentence includes words that appeal to the readers' sense of reason?
    (A) Giving every student a laptop computer to use at school would help our school save money in the long run.
    (B) Students at our school feel left behind without laptop computers.
    (C) Our school should be embarrassed by the fact that we have no laptop computer for students to use.

Unit 13
Writing Paragraphs

A common problem with word choice is using a word because you *think* you know its meaning but you are unsure of its exact meaning. If you are not completely sure of the meaning of a word, look up the word in a dictionary. Be especially careful with words that sound alike.

"Hamlet! You consult me with such hurtful remarks!" cried the queen. (wrong word choice—*consult* means "to look to for advice.")

"Hamlet! You **insult** me with such hurtful remarks!" cried the queen. (correct word choice—*insult* means "to speak to rudely.")

Is the underlined word used correctly in each sentence?

12. "You are to be commended for your bravery," declared King Arthur.
(A) Yes **(B)** No, change to *intended*

13. In the book *Cat, You Better Come Home,* the cat impairs constantly to be allowed outside.
(A) Yes **(B)** No, change to *pleads*

14. It was wise for Jack not to propose the giant at the top of the beanstalk.
(A) Yes **(B)** No, change to *provoke*

15. In the 1300s, a deadly epidemic called the bubonic plague swept across Europe, killing millions of people.
(A) Yes **(B)** No, change to *epicenter*

16. "Do not utter another word," summoned the teacher.
(A) Yes **(B)** No, change to *demanded*

17. Egyptian pharaohs believed that it was their destiny to live again after their deaths, so they had their bodies preserved.
(A) Yes **(B)** No, change to *perceived*

18. The Renaissance is resembled as one of the greatest periods in the history of art.
(A) Yes **(B)** No, change to *recognized*

19. The United Nations headquarters in New York City <u>accommodates</u> thousands of people.
(A) Yes
(B) No, change to *moderates*

20. Many modern tools have their origins in the ancient Greek <u>citizenship</u>.
(A) Yes
(B) No, change to *civilization*

21. Bristled feet are a special <u>adoption</u> geckos have that help them climb up smooth surfaces.
(A) Yes
(B) No, change to *adaptation*

22. The Julliard School in New York City is a well-known <u>academy</u> for the performing arts.
(A) Yes
(B) No, change to *academic*

23. Joseph Lister was <u>responsive</u> for an important medical discovery in the 1800s.
(A) Yes
(B) No, change to *responsible*

24. Koko the gorilla's <u>intention</u> was never to harm the kitten she dearly loved.
(A) Yes
(B) No, change to *interaction*

25. Peggy Fleming has been an <u>installation</u> for young ice skaters since the 1960s.
(A) Yes
(B) No, change to *inspiration*

Unit 14

Writing Paragraphs

Transitions

In paragraphs, **transition words** help your sentences flow smoothly and your ideas fit together clearly. Transition words can tell about time, location, order, and cause-and-effect relationships. They can also indicate how things are alike and how things are different.

First, find the Harper Street library. **Then,** use the driveway **between** the red lampposts. **Last,** go left **when** you see my apartment.

Which transition words best complete each paragraph?

To walk to the White House from the Lincoln Memorial, go two blocks north on 23rd Street (1) _____ you reach the intersection of 23rd and C Street. (2) _____ turn left on C Street, continue six blocks east, and turn left on 17th Street. (3) _____ you head north on 17th Street, you will see the White House grounds on your right. To reach the visitors' entrance, pass the White House, and turn right at Pennsylvania Avenue. (4) _____ walk to the entrance on your right.

1. **(A)** because **(B)** until **(C)** first
2. **(A)** Lastly **(B)** Finally **(C)** Then
3. **(A)** Until **(B)** Later **(C)** As
4. **(A)** Finally **(B)** Now **(C)** Secondly

There are four major tournaments in professional tennis. The (5) _____ tournament of the year, the Australian Open, is played in January. (6) _____, qualified players compete at the French Open in May. (7) _____ they play at Wimbledon, which is a tournament held in England every June. The (8) _____ major tournament of the year, the United States Open, takes place in August.

5. **(A)** last **(B)** final **(C)** first
6. **(A)** Next week **(B)** Four months later **(C)** At year's end
7. **(A)** The following month **(B)** When **(C)** Much later
8. **(A)** third **(B)** last **(C)** earliest

Unit 14
Writing Paragraphs

The life cycle of a fruit fly is (9) _____ the shortest on Earth. (10) _____ fruit fly eggs are laid, it takes just twenty-four hours for the eggs to hatch. A teeny wormlike creature called a larva then emerges from each egg. (11) _____ eight days, the larva has developed into a pupa. The pupa is in an inactive stage of development for six days, and (12) _____ an adult fruit fly emerges. By the end of two days, those adult females may lay eggs because they might live only one more week.

9.	**(A)** always	**(B)** never	**(C)** among
10.	**(A)** Before	**(B)** After	**(C)** Although
11.	**(A)** Across	**(B)** Within	**(C)** Throughout
12.	**(A)** while	**(B)** maybe	**(C)** then

In the year of 1776, San Francisco was founded by Spanish explorers and missionaries. (13) _____ Mexico won its independence from Spain in 1821, many Mexican farmers began to settle in California. Thus San Francisco became a small port town from which agricultural products were exported. Twenty-seven years (14) _____, California became part of the United States in 1848 after its victory in a war with Mexico. (15) _____, in 1849, gold was discovered in California, and San Francisco was transformed from a small port to a bustling city. (16) _____ a single year, San Francisco's population grew from eight hundred people to more than twenty-five thousand.

13.	**(A)** Now	**(B)** When	**(C)** Monthly
14.	**(A)** later	**(B)** before	**(C)** until
15.	**(A)** Prior to	**(B)** First	**(C)** Following that
16.	**(A)** Across	**(B)** Although	**(C)** Within

An infant wildebeest, a type of African antelope, can stand on its own legs just (17) _____ its birth. (18) _____ its mother cleans the newborn while it stands. (19) _____, a young wildebeest can run with the other herd members. (20) _____, the youngster will even be able to keep up with a herd's day-long journey.

17.	**(A)** as	**(B)** minutes after	**(C)** between
18.	**(A)** Soon	**(B)** Near	**(C)** When
19.	**(A)** Within an hour	**(B)** Again	**(C)** Whereas
20.	**(A)** Although	**(B)** Daily	**(C)** Surprisingly

Unit 15

Writing Paragraphs

Complete Paragraphs

A **complete paragraph** includes a topic sentence, related details, and a closing sentence. All sentences in a paragraph should support the topic, and there should be enough information to make your ideas clear. A complete paragraph should not have gaps that require a reader to fill in missing information. Thoughtful organization, staying on topic, and smooth transitions can help you write a strong and complete paragraph.

Which sentence correctly completes each paragraph?

1. The Leaning Tower of Pisa in Italy is an architectural wonder. The cylinder-shaped tower, which has eight stories extending one hundred and eighty-five feet, leans to one side. The tower's construction began in the year 1173. When the third story was completed about twenty years later, workers discovered that one side of the tower's base was sinking into the ground. After architects tried unsuccessfully to straighten the tower, construction resumed and continued for over two hundred years. _____

   (A) Once completed in the year 1360, the tower was still leaning, as it continues to do today.

   (B) Each bell in the tower has a different tone based on the musical scale.

   (C) The Leaning Tower is a popular image on Italian postcards.

---

2. By the time students reach middle or junior high school, they should be earning money by doing chores for family members and neighbors. Having responsibilities that depend on money helps students understand that money does not just appear. While money is earned and saved, students can learn to make better decisions about what is really worth buying. _____ Sometimes earning money even helps students with their math skills, as they calculate prices and tax.

   (A) Additionally, students can learn the importance of doing a job well and develop a sense of independence.

   (B) At any age, I would not consider an unsafe job as a way to earn money.

   (C) In general, watching television, playing video games, and surfing the Internet should be limited activities.

3. The respiratory system is what enables us to breathe. The process of breathing begins when air flows into the nose or mouth. The air enters the main part of a system of tubes called the *trachea,* travels through the *bronchi,* another system of tubes, and continues into the lungs. _____ Through the process of diffusion, oxygen exits the sacs to enter *capillaries,* the smallest of blood vessels, and begins to enrich the blood. Meanwhile, carbon dioxide diffuses in the lungs, moves up the bronchi and trachea, and is then exhaled through the nose or mouth.

(A) Blood is carried to all cells of the body through a variety of artery and capillary systems.

(B) While in the lungs, the oxygen in the air fills millions of tiny sacs.

(C) The *diaphragm* is a muscle located just below the lungs.

4. From the time the first English colonists landed in the 1600s, the United States has been a nation of immigrants. People from almost every part of the world have immigrated to the United States, making it the "melting pot" of the world. Some immigrants relocate to escape war, poverty, or other injustices of their homeland. _____ Collectively, immigrants offer a rich ethnic heritage in the United States.

(A) Other countries experience immigration on a smaller scale.

(B) Boats and airplanes are common modes of transportation.

(C) Other immigrants seek adventure, land, or opportunity.

5. In 1980, an earthquake shook Mount St. Helens, which is a volcanic mountain in the state of Washington. The earthquake triggered a major eruption of the volcano, and it spewed ash and smoke into the area. More than three hundred feet of the volcano's peak collapsed and exploded. An avalanche of debris covered the twenty-four square miles directly surrounding Mount St. Helens. _____

(A) Small-scale earthquakes that are not even felt by most people occur more than you might think.

(B) Scientists observe Mount St. Helens from a nearby observatory.

(C) An additional two hundred and fifty square miles of land was severely damaged by the eruption.

Unit 15
Writing Paragraphs

Which sentence correctly completes each paragraph?

6. A person who lives alone should consider getting a dog for a pet. A dog can help prevent the feeling of loneliness and sometimes depression. ____ Medical studies have shown that the contact, love, and loyalty of a dog can lower an owner's blood pressure. Finally, many dogs can provide a sense of security to those who live alone.

(A) A dog should get daily exercise and never be left in a vehicle alone no matter what the temperature.

(B) Having a dog to walk helps an owner stay active and meet other people, if that is what the owner chooses.

(C) From what I have heard, a cat does not like to wear a leash to go for a walk.

---

7. On Africa's western coast lies The Namib Desert, the oldest desert in the world. ____ The desert contains the highest sand dunes in the world; some rise to a height of over one thousand feet. Though the Namib Desert covers more than one hundred thousand square miles, there is little vegetation due to the severe climate. Fog along the desert's coast once caused numerous shipwrecks, which is why it is nicknamed "The Skeleton Coast."

(A) Most of the Namib Desert is located in the African country of Namibia.

(B) The Atlantic Ocean surrounds Africa on the west.

(C) Typically, hot deserts experience significantly cooler temperatures at night.

---

8. I just completed a painting that I have been working on for seven weeks. ____ In the foreground, the painting's focal point is a medieval castle. The castle has four round towers, two on each side at the front and the rear. A wide and murky moat encircles the castle. For the castle's only entrance, there is a drawbridge lowered over the moat. Grasses, wildflowers, trees, and shrubs surround the moat.

(A) Watercolors can be difficult because they tend to drip and smear.

(B) My sister and I are going to take a sculpting class together.

(C) Misty mountains and gray clouds form my painting's background.

9. The fifty United States took nearly two hundred years to establish. The first colonies were founded from the early 1600s to the mid 1700s; their statehood would follow much later. Gradually, settled territories were added almost yearly until 1822, which began a fifteen-year period without any new states. _____ Finally, Hawaii and Alaska were the last states to enter the Union in 1959.

(A) In 1836, Arkansas became a state, and the trend started again.
(B) Missouri was the twenty-fourth state to join the Union.
(C) Texas and Florida became states in the same year.

---

10. Iceboats are designed to travel across ice at high speeds. _____ A single sail hangs from a mast in front of the cockpit. An iceboat's cockpit holds one or two people. Three steel runners are attached lengthwise to the boat's base; one at the front steers the boat. Iceboats can travel as fast as one hundred miles per hour.

(A) An iceboat's long hull is made of light wood, aluminum, or fiberglass.
(B) An iceboat's crew wears spiked footwear to grip ice as they walk.
(C) Fiberglass consists mainly of special fibers and plastic.

---

11. Geckos are small lizards that live in warm climates. Their eyes are covered by transparent eyelids that always stay closed. Each of a gecko's tiny toes ends in a circular pad with thousands of bristles. _____ Geckos can walk upside down on the bottom of just about anything!

(A) An alligator is not the same as a crocodile.
(B) These pads help geckos perform an amazing and unusual task.
(C) Amphibians are cold-blooded, which means their temperature is based on their environment.

---

12. _____ Tortillas are thin, flat pieces of bread that are made from corn flour. Tacos, enchiladas, chimichangas, and burritos all use tortillas prepared differently. These breads can be stuffed with a variety of ingredients, such as rice, beans, cheese, onions, lettuce, and peppers. Tortillas are also used to make *quesadillas*, or Mexican pizzas.

(A) Italian and Mexican meals are my top two favorites.
(B) Mexico borders the United States to the south.
(C) Tortillas are the central part of most Mexican meals.

The Last LAP
Language Activity Pages

A. Exercising Your Skill

You have been learning about descriptive writing in paragraphs, including similes, metaphors, personification, and exaggeration. You have learned about word choice and transition words. In addition, you have reinforced your knowledge of how to write a complete paragraph. Number your paper from 1 to 10. Read the sentences below. Use a word from the box only once to complete each sentence correctly.

expository	simile	audience	Exaggeration	metaphor
Transitions	Personification	dialogue	Organization	descriptive

1. A _____ compares two different things without using *like* or *as*.
2. A _____ compares two different things with the word *like* or *as*.
3. _____ help a paragraph and its ideas flow smoothly.
4. The goal of _____ writing is to develop a vivid image for the reader.
5. _____ compares ideas or objects as if they have human qualities.
6. _____ is figurative language that stretches the truth.
7. Time and order words help clarify the steps of a process in _____ writing.
8. In persuasive writing, choose words that will affect your _____ the most.
9. In narrative writing, use _____ that is true to its characters.
10. _____ that is thoughtful can help you write a strong and complete paragraph.

B. Expanding Your Skill

Number your paper from 1 to 5. Read the paragraph below. Some figurative language is missing from it. On your paper, write a word or a phrase from the box only once to complete each description.

a chance in a million	buckets	like the wind	moaned	angry

While strolling back to the cabin, we noticed that dark, (1) _____ clouds were gathering on the horizon. A sudden gust blew away my scarf; I did not have (2) _____ of catching it. As the storm's downpour began, we ran (3) _____ to get to the cabin. We arrived just in time! The wooden door slammed shut behind us, and (4) _____ of rain continued to fall. The old roof (5) _____ from the storm's force.

C. Exploring Language

Descriptive Writing Number your paper from 1 to 5. Read the paragraph below to answer the questions that follow.

Sunset Dance—Ceremony to the Evening Sun is a beautiful painting on display at the National Museum of American Art. Joseph Henry Sharp painted it in 1924. Grouped in various areas outside the pueblos of a village, Native Americans in the painting are dressed in brightly colored clothes. The museum in our town is closed on Thursdays and Sundays, but is open longer during the rest of the week. Standing behind a low wall of a pueblo in the foreground, there are some people with their backs to the viewer. There are two groups of people crowded in front of a ceremonial wall that arches squarely above them. **Lastly, the painting's background shows purple and blue mountains.** This painting inspires because of its tribute to heritage.

1. Which of these sentences is the paragraph's topic sentence?
   (A) Joseph Henry Sharp painted it in 1924.
   (B) *Sunset Dance—Ceremony to the Evening Sun* is a beautiful painting on display at the National Museum of American Art.
2. Does the underlined sentence support the paragraph's topic?
   (A) Yes **(B)** No
3. Choose the *most* descriptive word to replace the underlined word.
   (A) other **(B)** more **(C)** three
4. Does the boldfaced sentence include a transition word?
   (A) Yes **(B)** No
5. Which of these sentences is the paragraph's closing sentence?
   (A) This painting inspires because of its tribute to heritage.
   (B) Lastly, the painting's background shows purple and blue mountains.

D. Expressing Yourself

Choose one of these activities. When you are finished, give your paper to your teacher.

1. Tall tales often use exaggeration to make them humorous. Write your own tall tale that includes funny examples of exaggeration.
2. WORK with a PARTNER With a partner, write a poem about nature. Use at least one metaphor, one simile, and one example of personification.

PARAGRAPHS Scope and Sequence • *Specific Skill Series for Language Arts*

Unit/Level	Level A	Level B	Level C	Level D	Level E	Level F	Level G	Level H
Unit 1	Types of Paragraphs	Types of Paragraphs	Types of Paragraphs	Types of Paragraphs	Narrative Paragraphs	Narrative Paragraphs	Narrative Paragraphs	Narrative Paragraphs
Unit 2	Types of Paragraphs	Using a Web	Using a Web	Using a Web	Narrative Paragraphs	Narrative Paragraphs	Narrative Paragraphs	Narrative Paragraphs
Unit 3	Using a Web	Topic Sentences	Topic Sentences	Topic Sentences	Narrative Paragraphs	Narrative Paragraphs	Narrative Paragraphs	Narrative Paragraphs
Unit 4	Topic Sentences	Details	Details	Details	Narrative Paragraphs	Narrative Paragraphs	Narrative Paragraphs	Narrative Paragraphs
Unit 5	Topic Sentences	Closing Sentences	Closing Sentences	Closing Sentences	Persuasive Paragraphs	Persuasive Paragraphs	Persuasive Paragraphs	Persuasive Paragraphs
Unit 6	Details	Complete Paragraphs	Complete Paragraphs	Complete Paragraphs	Persuasive Paragraphs	Persuasive Paragraphs	Persuasive Paragraphs	Persuasive Paragraphs
Unit 7	Closing Sentences	Staying on Topic	Staying on Topic	Staying on Topic	Persuasive Paragraphs	Persuasive Paragraphs	Persuasive Paragraphs	Persuasive Paragraphs
Unit 8	Complete Paragraphs	Time and Order Words	Time and Order Words	Transition Words	Expository Paragraphs	Expository Paragraphs	Persuasive Paragraphs	Persuasive Paragraphs
Unit 9	Staying on Topic	Using Dialogue	Using Dialogue	Sentence Variety	Expository Paragraphs	Expository Paragraphs	Expository Paragraphs	Expository Paragraphs
Unit 10	Time and Order Words	Making Comparisons	Making Comparisons	Using Dialogue	Expository Paragraphs	Expository Paragraphs	Expository Paragraphs	Expository Paragraphs
Unit 11				Figurative Language	Writing Paragraphs	Writing Paragraphs	Expository Paragraphs	Expository Paragraphs
Unit 12					Writing Paragraphs	Writing Paragraphs	Writing Paragraphs	Writing Paragraphs
Unit 13					Writing Paragraphs	Writing Paragraphs	Writing Paragraphs	Writing Paragraphs
Unit 14					Writing Paragraphs	Writing Paragraphs	Writing Paragraphs	Writing Paragraphs
Unit 15					Writing Paragraphs	Writing Paragraphs	Writing Paragraphs	Writing Paragraphs
Unit 16							Writing Paragraphs	Writing Paragraphs